D0889940

The Story of Our Holidays

HANUKKAH

Joanna Ponto and Arlene Erlbach

Enslow Publishing
101 W. 23rd Street
Suite 240
New York, NY 10011
USA

enslow.com

Published in 2017 by Enslow Publishing, LLC.
101 W. 23rd Street, Suite 240, New York, NY 10011

Library of Congress Cataloging-in-Publication Data
Names: Ponto, Joanna, author. | Erlbach, Arlene, author.
Title: Hanukkah / Joanna Ponto and Arlene Erlbach.
Description: New York, NY : Enslow Publishing, [2017] | Series: The Story of Our Holidays | Grades 4-6. | Includes bibliographical references and index.
Identifiers: LCCN 2016001034| ISBN 9780766076280 (library bound) | ISBN 9780766076259 (pbk.) | ISBN 9780766076266 (6-pack)
Subjects: LCSH: Hanukkah--Juvenile literature.
Classification: LCC BM695.H3 P66 2016 | DDC 296.4/35--dc23
LC record available at http://lccn.loc.gov/2016001034

Printed in the United States of America

To Our Readers: We have done our best to make sure all website addresses in this book were active and appropriate when we went to press. However, the author and the publisher have no control over and assume no liability for the material available on those websites or on any websites they may link to. Any comments or suggestions can be sent by e-mail to customerservice@enslow.com.

Portions of this book originally appeared in the book *Hanukkah: Celebrating the Holiday of Lights* by Arlene Erlbach.

Photo Credits: Cover, Daniel Hurst Photography/Photographer's Choice RF/Getty Images; p. 4 Andy Cripe/The Corvallis Gazette-Times/AP Photo; p. 7 Noam Armonn/Hemera/Thinkstock; p. 8 Lisa J Goodman/Moment Mobile/Getty Images; p. 10 Menahem Kahana/AFP/Getty Images; p. 11 Sean Pavone/Shutterstock.com; p. 14 david156/Shutterstock.com; p. 16 Print Collector/Hulton Archive/Getty Images; p. 20 Jani Bryson/iStock/Thinkstock; p. 21 Stephen Chernin/Getty Images; p. 24 Derek Hatfield/Shutterstock.com; p. 25 Olaf Speier/Shutterstock.com; p. 26 Fuse/Thinkstock; p. 29 © Karen Huang.

Craft created by Sophie Hayn and Aniya Strickland.

Contents

Jewish people everywhere celebrate Hanukkah, the festival of lights.

Chapter 1

A Festival of Lights

Hanukkah is a very happy holiday that is celebrated by Jewish people around the world. Hanukkah begins on the eve of the twenty-fifth day of the Hebrew month called Kislev, which is either November or December in the Western calendar. It lasts for eight days and nights.

Lighting the Menorah

Jewish people sometimes attend parties during Hanukkah. They may play games, eat special foods, sing songs, and give gifts. On each night of Hanukkah, families burn candles in a candleholder called a menorah. A menorah has places for nine candles.

One of the nine candles is the *shamash*, which means "helper" in Hebrew. It is lit first and is used to light the other eight candles. On the first night, the shamash is used to light one candle. On the second night, the shamash is used to light two candles. On the third night, three candles are lit with the shamash.

A Calendar Based on the Moon Rebirth

A traditional Jewish calendar is different from the calendar we use every day. The calendar we use is based on the cycles of the sun. Each year has 365 days because it takes 365 days for the earth to move completely around the sun. A traditional Jewish calendar is based on the moon. Each month begins when there is a new moon in the sky, and each month has a Hebrew name.

The lighting of one more candle each night goes on until all of the candles are lit on the last night. Another name for Hanukkah is "Festival of Lights."

Hanukkah's Origins

Hanukkah comes around the same time of the year that Christians celebrate Christmas. But Hanukkah and Christmas are very different holidays. Hanukkah gives thanks for a battle that the Jewish people won more than two thousand years ago against the ancient Greeks. The Greeks, who ruled over the Jews at the time,

Each night during Hanukkah, families gather together to light their menorah.

told the Jews that they could not practice their religion. They were not allowed to pray in the temple, their place of worship.

After winning their fight with the Greeks, the Jewish people took back the temple. Then they rededicated it to God. The word "Hanukkah" means "dedication."

Hanukkah is celebrated with parties and food. But there is a deeper meaning to the holiday.

Chapter 2

Understanding Judaism

The Jewish people follow one of the oldest religions in the world. This religion is called Judaism. Judaism is more than five thousand years old, according to the Jewish calendar.

An Ancient Religion

Judaism is the first religion to teach that there is only one God. A wise man named Abraham is considered the father of the Jewish people. Moses is another well-known Jewish person. According to the Bible, God wrote and then gave Moses the Ten Commandments. They are a list of rules for living and for worshipping. One of the commandments tells people to honor their father and mother.

Jewish people worship in a temple or synagogue. In some branches, men and women are separated .

Like all religions, Judaism follows certain customs. Jewish people call the places where they pray temples or synagogues. They call their religious leaders rabbis. Jewish people use only the Tanakh—the Hebrew Bible. The Old Testament is based on the Hebrew Bible.

Some Jewish Customs

Some Jewish people follow certain rules about what they can and cannot eat. These people do not eat pork or shellfish. They do not eat dairy products when they eat meat or poultry. They eat only food that is kosher. This means that the food has been prepared in a certain way.

Jewish people observe their Sabbath from Friday evening at sundown until Saturday at sundown. Many Jews celebrate the Sabbath in their home with a special meal. They may also go to temple for prayer services. Some Jews do not work, drive cars, use electricity, or spend money during the Sabbath. This time is meant to be a day of prayer, rest, and study of Judaism.

There are more than 14 million Jews in the world. Many of them live in the United States. But Jews have also had their own country,

Israel is the national state of the Jewish people. However, Jews live in countries around the world.

The Western Wall

Jews from around the world travel to Israel to pray at the Western Wall in Jerusalem. Israel is a country in the Middle East that many Jewish people call home. The Western Wall is the holiest place for Jews to pray.

called Israel, since 1948. Its capital city is Jerusalem, and its official language is Hebrew. Many Jewish people who live in North America can read and speak Hebrew, too. Jewish children may be taught Hebrew at religious schools.

Life and Growth

Hanukkah honors the Jewish people's victory over the ancient Greeks. But other enemies have also tried to destroy the Jewish people. More than three thousand years ago, the Egyptians kept Jews as slaves. The spring holiday of Passover celebrates the release of the Jews from slavery. During World War II (from 1939 to 1945), German Nazis killed more than 6 million Jews.

In spite of enemies who have tried to destroy them throughout history, the Jewish people have continued to live and grow. Hanukkah is a happy reminder of that life and growth.

Chapter 3

The First Hanukkah

In ancient times, the land the Jewish people lived in was called Palestine, or Judea. During that time, this part of the world was captured and ruled by many different people.

The Eternal Light

The capital city was, and still is, Jerusalem. It is the most holy city in Israel. The Temple was located there. The Temple was the religious center for the Jewish people. They would visit the Temple and pray to their God. In the Temple, there was a special oil lamp that was always kept lit. It was used to light all the other sacred lights in the Temple.

The priests were the men who took care of the Temple. They made sure the Eternal Light never went out. They kept the lamp filled with special oil that they made from olives. It took more than a week to make the oil. No other oil could be used.

Under Greek Rule

Around the year 330 BCE the Greeks took over Palestine. The religious beliefs of the Greek people were different from those of the Jews. The Greeks did not believe in only one god. They believed that many gods controlled the world. They prayed to statues of these gods. The statues were called idols.

Olive oil was kept in pitchers like this and used to fill lamps.

Even though the Greeks had different religious beliefs, they let the Jews pray in peace. Some Jewish people liked the Greek way of life better than the Jewish way of life. They began to practice the Greek customs. Other Jewish people followed their own customs.

In 175 BCE a new king, King Antiochus IV, began ruling Palestine. He told the Jews they had to give up their religion. He wanted all Jews to be like the Greeks in every way.

The new king would not allow Jewish religious services to be held. He destroyed religious objects in the Temple in Jerusalem. He replaced them with statues of Greek gods. He ordered the Jews to pray to these statues. If the Jews refused, they would be killed. The king sold some of the Jewish people who did not obey into slavery.

Some Jews tried to escape the king's rules by moving away. But they could not hide from the king's soldiers. The soldiers found the Jews who were trying to hide and forced them to give up their religion.

The Maccabean Revolt

In 167 BCE some of the king's soldiers came to the village of Modiin. There, the soldiers built a statue of Zeus, the king of the Greek gods. The soldiers put a pig near the statue. Then, they forced the men of the town to stand near the statue.

The Jewish leader of Modiin was an old man named Mattathias. The king's soldiers ordered Mattathias to kill the pig and eat it. Mattathias stayed true to his religion and refused.

One man offered to do what the soldiers wanted. Mattathias killed the man and the Greek leader of the soldiers. Then Mattathias, his five sons, and other Jews in the village killed the rest of the soldiers.

Mattathias and his men left their village and hid in the mountains.

Sometimes they came down from the mountains to attack the king's men. They also smashed statues of the Greek gods.

The Maccabean Revolt is a reminder of the strength of the Jewish people.

They asked people to join them. Many Jewish people joined with Mattathias and his men.

The rebellion lasted for about two years. Mattathias died during the first year. Before his death, his son Judah took over. Judah and his men kept fighting even when things looked hopeless. They continued to hammer away at their enemy. Judah and his men became known as the Maccabees. Maccabee means "hammer." This event began what is known as the Maccabean Revolt.

A Miracle

The king's army was larger than the Jewish army. The Maccabees had only a few thousand soldiers. The king's army had many thousands of men and more effective weapons. The king's men had bows and arrows. The Maccabees had only sticks, stones, and farm tools. Judah Maccabee was a great leader. He and his soldiers believed that God would help them win.

The Maccabees won three battles against the king's troops. The king thought he would finally win if he led a fourth battle. He got together more than twenty-five thousand men, but the Maccabees won again. Then the Maccabees marched to Jerusalem to fix the

A Long Fight

King Antiochus IV, who fought against Judah and the Maccabees, died the year after the first Hanukkah. But the Jews continued to fight battles with the king's followers for about twenty years. Judah died in one of those battles. Jonathan, Mattathias's youngest son, took over. But he, too, was killed. Finally, Simon, the oldest son, forced the invaders out. Israel stayed free for more than one hundred years.

damage that was done to the Temple.

Judah Maccabee and his men removed the statues of the Greek gods from the Temple. They cleaned off dirt and blood that was on the walls. Then Judah went to light the special oil lamp that was supposed to stay lit all the time. It is said that Judah found only enough oil for the light to last for one day. It would take longer than that to make more oil. By what appeared to be a miracle, the oil lasted for all eight days. Judah was able to prepare more oil so the lamp would not go out again. This was the first Hanukkah.

Judah Maccabee and his people had started a new holiday for the Jewish people. It would be celebrated every year and would last for eight days and nights. That holiday is called Hanukkah.

Chapter 4

Lighting the Menorah

One of the best known symbols of Hanukkah is the menorah. *Menorah* is a Hebrew word that means "lamp." The special kind of menorah used during Hanukkah is called a hanukkiah.

A hanukkiah contains nine candleholders. One of the holders is for the shamash candle. This is the candle that is used to light the rest of the candles. The other candles stand for each night of the miracle of the oil. Only the shamash can be used to light these candles.

The candles of the menorah are lit from left to right.
Kids may take turns lighting the candles each night.

Special Rules

There is a certain way to light a menorah. On the first night of Hanukkah, the candle in the holder farthest to the right is lit. Each night another candle is placed in the menorah and lit until the eighth night, when all of the candles in the menorah are lit.

The candles are always added from right to left and lit from left to right. Each night a special prayer is said while lighting the candles.

Eternal lights are displayed in all synagogues, like this one in New York City.

The Eternal Light

Today all temples and synagogues contain a light that always burns, much like the light in the first Temple in Jerusalem. This light is known as the Eternal Light.

The candles in the menorah should be allowed to burn for at least half an hour and should not be blown out. Hanukkah candles are special and should be used only in a menorah. They are a reminder for everyone of the miracle of the holiday.

Many families put the menorah near a window for everyone to see. In many families, people take turns lighting the candles. Sometimes everyone has his or her own menorah.

Chapter 5

Hanukkah Parties

For Jewish children, Hanukkah is one of the most exciting times of the year. They look forward to Hanukkah gifts, games, parties, and special foods.

Hanukkah Gifts

Many children receive *gelt*, or money, as a gift. Some children receive gifts on each of the eight nights of Hanukkah. Some families give gifts to each other on only one night. For some families Hanukkah is a time to give gifts to those who are more needy than they are.

The gift-giving part of Hanukkah is not an original custom of the holiday. However, it has become a part of celebrating

Hanukkah for many Jewish families. The way families give gifts to each other is different from family to family.

Treats

Hanukkah parties can happen on any night of the holiday. Families and friends gather to share the joy of the holiday together. Foods

Many children receive chocolate treats, called Hanukkah gelt, made to look like coins.

such as latkes, or potato pancakes, are served, often accompanied by applesauce. A recipe for applesauce appears on the next page. The latkes are fried in oil as a way of remembering the oil from the Temple in Jerusalem.

Hanukkah Applesauce*

6 cups apple, peeled, cored, and cut into bite-sized pieces (Use tart apples such as Granny Smiths, Fujis, or some combination of the two. You don't want the applesauce to be too sweet.)

¾ cup cold water
1 teaspoon ground cinnamon
¼ teaspoon each: ground cloves, ginger, and nutmeg
Juice of ½ a lemon
½ cup sugar

Directions:

1. In a large saucepan over medium heat, combine apples, water, spices, and lemon juice.
2. Bring to a boil.
3. Reduce heat and simmer until apples soften. Remove from heat.
4. With a large spoon or potato masher, mash the apples until a thick paste has formed.
5. Stir in the sugar and return to heat. Simmer for five more minutes or until sugar has dissolved.
6. Enjoy over latkes, roast chicken, or just on its own!

* Adult supervision required.

Some families eat jelly doughnuts called *sufganiyot*. These, too, are fried in oil.

Hanukkah Games

A dreidel is a toy that looks like a top. It has four sides with a different Hebrew letter printed on each side. These letters are called: nun, gimel, hei, and shin. They stand for a phrase that means "a great miracle happened here." Each letter also stands for an activity in the dreidel game.

Spinning the dreidel is a fun Hanukkah activity for kids and adults alike. Kids often play the dreidel game at parties.

Many people begin the dreidel game by putting a penny, dime, nut, or piece of candy in the center of an imaginary circle. Then each player takes a turn spinning the dreidel. Depending on which letter the dreidel lands, the player takes everything in the center, adds one piece to the center, takes half of what is in the center, or does nothing.

Different families have their own special ways of playing the dreidel game. Gambling is not allowed in the Jewish religion, but the dreidel game is a fun way to remember the miracle of Hanukkah. No matter how a family celebrates Hanukkah, the lighting of the menorah is at the center of the holiday.

Fun with Dreidels

Hanukkah is a fun holiday for Jewish children. They can go to parties, light the menorah, and eat special foods. They also get treats and play the dreidel game.

Hanukkah Craft*

Have fun playing the dreidel game! First you will learn how to make your own dreidel. Then you will find out how to play the game.

Here are the supplies you will need:

a ruler
a sharp pencil
construction paper that is at
   least 5 inches (12.7 cm) long
   on all sides
safety scissors
markers
tape

Directions:

1. Use the ruler and the pencil to measure and draw the outline of a five-inch by five-inch square on the construction paper.

2. Cut the square out of the construction paper.

3. Fold the points of the square that are opposite each other toward the center of the square.

4. Use the markers to print these words for Hebrew letters on each flap of the dreidel: nun, gimel, hei, shin.

5. Insert a pencil into the center of your folded dreidel with the point of the pencil facing the ground.

6. Tape the pencil securely to the dreidel.

Make a Dreidel

How to Play:

1. Every player puts in the center a piece of candy, nut, raisin, penny, or another small object.

2. Each player takes turns spinning the pencil attached to the dreidel.

3. When the dreidel lands on nun, that player takes nothing out of the center.

4. When the dreidel lands on gimel, that player takes everything from the center.

5. When the dreidel lands on hei, that player takes half of what is in the center.

6. When the dreidel lands on shin, that player puts one game piece in the center.

7. Whenever the center is empty, everyone puts in one game piece.

The game is played until one player has won all of the pieces.

*Safety note: Be sure to ask for help from an adult, if needed, to complete this project.

29

Glossary

dreidel—A small toy top with Hebrew letters on each side.

Hebrew—The language spoken by the ancient Jews. It is still spoken and learned by many Jews today.

Judaism—The religion of the Jews. It is based on a belief in one god and the teachings of the Old Testament.

kosher—Food that is prepared according to Jewish ceremonial law.

latkes—Potato pancakes that are fried in oil.

menorah—A candleholder used by the Jewish people at Hanukkah.

rabbi—A Jewish religious leader who teaches the laws and customs of Judaism.

Sabbath—The day of the week that is used for worship. Saturday is the Sabbath for the Jews.

shamash—The candle in the Hanukkah menorah that is used to light all of the other candles.

sufganiyot—Jelly-filled doughnuts.

Learn More

Books

Dickmann, Nancy. *Hanukkah.* Oxford, England: Raintree, 2012.

Herrington, Lisa M. *Hanukkah.* New York, NY: Children's Press, 2014.

Keogh, Josie. *Hanukkah.* New York, NY: PowerKids Press, 2013.

Trueit, Trudi Strain, and Rebecca McKillip Thornburgh. *Hanukkah.* Mankato, MN: Child's World, 2014.

Websites

Billy Bear's Hanukkah

billybear4kids.com/holidays/hanukkah/hanukkah.htm
Enjoy plenty of Hanukkah crafts and games on this site.

DLTK's Hanukkah Crafts for Kids

dltk-kids.com/world/jewish/hanukah.htm
Learn how to make a menorah out of marshmallows, have fun with coloring pages, or do an online Hanukkah jigsaw puzzle.

The Holiday Spot: Hanukkah Celebrations

theholidayspot.com/hanukkah
Learn the history of Hanukkah, send cards to your friends, and make tasty holiday recipes!

Index